LET'S START
BREAKERS

KV-191-218

THE HEAVIEST LIVING LAND ANIMAL

Average weight 5.7 tonnes.

You'll see several differences between the two elephants here and on page 4. (1) is African; (2) is Indian.

African Elephant (1) The largest living land mammal. A full-grown bull may be 4 metres tall at the shoulders, weigh more than 6 tonnes, and have 2.4 metres tusks. (The longest tusk on record is 2.71 metres, 133 kg.) Look at his outward sloping forehead, very large ears and the inward curve on the back. The trunk, which is like a series of telescopic rings, ends with two finger-like points. (Very large ears, remember.)

Indian Elephant (2) Smaller than his African cousin, with smaller ears, smoother trunk, and a high domed forehead. The trunk ends with a single 'finger' tip. Females are tuskless or have small tusks which can't be seen from the exterior.

Which type of elephant did you see? ....
....Score **30**

(1)

THE SMALLEST LIVING LAND ANIMAL

Well there's still a bit of an argument. Some say the Etruscan Shrew holds the record. You could get 2,850,000 average Etruscan Shrews for the weight of an average African Elephant.

How much does an average Etruscan Shrew weigh? ....Score **30**

You will be lucky to see one of the shrews, so which type of shrew did you spy? ....
....Score **30**

NB: TREE SHREWS AND ELEPHANT SHREWS DON'T COUNT

Others say the smallest is the Tiny Pipistrelle Bat from W. Africa, for its average weight is much the same as the Etruscan Shrew (have you worked it out yet?). New animals are still being discovered in places like S.E. Asia, and the record may go to another.

Bats There are 1000 species in the world, most of which live in the tropics and warmer parts. They are mammals which have adapted to fly, and they cannot walk. The body may be 2.5–30 cm long, their wingspan as much as 1.5 metres. In the wild they have 1–2 babies in spring, which cling to the mother's breast with their hooked teeth. She carries them as she flies for the first few weeks then leaves them hanging upon the nest.

Most bats are insectivorous, feeding on moths, beetles and other night-flying insects. Some catch fish and 2 kinds are carnivorous: they eat rodents, frogs and other bats. The large **Fruit Bats** (3) hang in trees rather than caves, have different wings, ears and tails.

Vampire Bat (4) It lives on fresh blood which it laps from a cut it has made in the skin of living animals – horses, mules or even man. It's teeth are quite small, apart from 2 sharp incisors on the top. It lives in caves or holes in the tree in tropical Central and S. America.

As you are unlikely to see the smallest bat in captivity, which bat did you see? ....
....Score **30**

(3)

(4)

Cheetah (5) by name, by nature it doesn't have to cheat to win a race because it is the world record breaker. 100 kms an hour.

Man's fastest running speed is about 35 kms an hour; greyhounds can run at about 104 kms an hour; but the cheetah is the fastest of all animals. Starting from rest, a cheetah can reach 72 kms per hour in two seconds and then go on to speeds of up to 112 kms per hour. To help him run so fast the cheetah is the only member of the cat family to have permanently extended claws.

Cheetahs live on open grassland or scrub and move about by day in pairs or family parties. They live up to 16 years.

Cheetahs, although easily tamed and trained, are hard to breed in captivity. Whipsnade Zoo, however, has, over the years, bred 471 cheetah cubs – a world record.

At which zoo did you see a cheetah? ....
....Score **30**

chester

THE SLOWEST

The two-toed Sloth (6) travels at 0.1 kms an hour. Here is an animal that really hangs about. It lives among the trees, hanging beneath them, its back downwards and clinging with hooklike organs which are all the 'hands' its got. It has difficulty walking on the ground, and only moves slowly in the trees. But it can occasionally travel fast along the branches by making use of the swaying of boughs by the wind to cross larger gaps.

It eats leaves, young shoots, and fruits. It comes out at night, is alone and silent. There is one young born at a time.

Sloths can have 2 toes on the forefoot and 3 behind, or 3 on each foot.

(5)

(6)

THE HIGHEST LIVER

Yak (7) An ox-like animal from the mountains of Tibet and China. It grazes at 6,100 metres. There they are kept as beasts of burden; for riding; and for their milk, which the Tibetans make into butter. The shaggy coat hangs to the ankles, and the smooth black horns may be I metre long.

The longest living

Believe it or not, that record goes to a human being, Mrs. Delina Filkins, who lived to be almost 114 years of age. People also hold another less enviable record, they are without doubt the MOST DESTRUCTIVE MAMMAL.

(7)

Enough records for now, for these seven sorts of animals, all of which can be seen in zoos, introduces us to seven of the great groups of mammals and to the study of ZOOGEOGRAPHY, no not where our zoos are located but from where the animals they contain had their origins.

MAMMALS (warm-blooded, fur-bearing, milk-producing) are divided into groups:–

Lay eggs	Monotremes
Pouched	Marsupials
Insect Eaters	Insectivores
Gnawing	Rodents
Nibbling	Lagomorphs
Flesh Eaters	Carnivores
Fin-footed	Pinnipedia
Hoofed Feet	Perissodactyles
Cloven Feet	Artiodactyles
Thick skins, trunks, tusks	Elephants
Big Brains	Primates

They live in areas of the World which can be divided up as follows:-
1. New World tropical
2. New World arctic
3. Old World arctic
4. Ethiopian
5. Oriental
6. Australasian.
As you go round the zoos, check out the labels on the animals' homes, they will tell you the country of origin.

Perhaps the world's best known zoogeographical fact is that Kangaroos live in Australia.

Most of the native mammals found in Australasia are Pouch-bearers (Marsupials) and Egg-layers (Monotremes).

Duck-billed Platypus (8) so called because of the unique mouth parts. The young are hatched from eggs but then take milk from the mother like other mammals. There are normally 2 eggs at one time, laid at the far end of a burrow with an under-water entrance from a river or lake bank.

It can swim of course, and has webbed feet and a broad flat tail. The body is mole-like and ears and eyes small.

What other Monotreme do you know?..............
..Score **30**

Wallabies (9) and Kangaroos (10) are Marsupials. Their young are helpless for some time after birth and are carried in a pouch on the mother's abdomen. You'll see many species, ranging in size from the tiny tree-kangaroos, through the wallabies to the huge true kangaroos. They live on the Australian continent, Tasmania and New Guinea.

Kangaroo The Great Red Kangaroo is the largest marsupial; an old male may be more than 2 metres tall. When in a hurry he can bound along at 48 kms an hour making leaps of 10 metres.

Wallaby Rather like a small kangaroo. Those with hind feet less than 15cm long are generally

Grey Kangaroo;
　　Bennett's wallaby and its
　　　　　baby (Joey)

called scrub wallabies; larger species are called
brush wallabies.
What kind of marsupial did you see? ....
....Score **50**

The nibblers. Gnawing animals with 2 pairs of ever-growing teeth, a group which includes the very successful rabbits.

RODENTS. Also gnawing animals but with only 1 pair of front teeth. They are continuously replaced as they are worn down.

Agouti A fast-moving, long-legged rodent from Central and South America. Watch him pick up food with his forepaws, then sit back on his haunches to eat it.

Capybara (11) With an overall length of about four feet, he's the largest living rodent (which makes him the largest of 1,729 species). Always lives near water, and has slightly webbed feet.

There are about 200 species of squirrels of many sizes and colours. Two to watch for at the zoo are **Prevost's Squirrel** (12), from Malaya, and the **Malabar Giant Squirrel** from India. The Malabar is the biggest squirrel of all (his overall length is almost 1 metre).

A fascinating species of squirrel to look out for are the flying squirrels. They have a web of skin between the fore and hind limbs which is used for gliding from one tree to another.

What was the most interesting squirrel you saw? ....
....Score **20**

Beaver (13) A large rodent which spends most of his time in the water. The beaver's hind feet are webbed for swimming and his flat tail acts as a rudder (and as an alarm; he beats the water with it when afraid). He has very strong sharp teeth which he uses to chop down trees, to make his home (or lodge), and dams.

(11)

(13)

(12)

(14)

There are still many beavers in North America, and some can still be seen in Scandinavia and parts of Europe. They were once quite common in England.

I-SPYed a beaver at ....Score **20**

Porcupine (14) There are several species, all about the size of a badger. Tiny ears, short legs and a thumb on the forefeet. The quills stand up and rattle. Nocturnal and solitary.

Which species was your porcupine? ....
....Score **50**

Carnivore means meat-eaters, and there are very many flesh-eating mammals.

Hyrax (15) A puzzle for zoologists. He's only as big as a rabbit, but his nearest relatives appear to be the rhinoceros and the elephant. His front feet have four short hoof-like toes; his hind feet have three of them.

What colour was the fur of the hyrax you saw?

....Score **40**

Red Panda (16) From the Himalayas and the mountains of western China. I-SPY a woolly chestnut-red coat, long bushy tail, and a white face with black markings. He walks with a waddling movement.

I saw a Red Panda at.............................. *zoo*

....Score **40**

Brown Bear (17) Not always brown – he may be any colour from almost pure white to jet black. Once found throughout Europe (even in Britain), this was the dancing bear kept by showmen. The Kodiac Bear from Alaska, the biggest living land carnivore, and the American Grizzly are both thought to be races of Brown Bear. The Kodiac may stand 3 metres high and weigh up to 760 Kg.

American Black Bear (18) Not always black – you may see one that's brown. He is smaller, however, than the true Brown Bear and more rounded in shape. In the wild his diet is astonishing – wasp's nests, small mammals, grasses briars, roots, acorns, even pine cones. The bearskins worn by British Guardsmen were made from his fur.

Which bear did you see, and where?.................

....Score **20**

(15)

(16)

(17)

(18)

Tiger (19) Although the lion is reckoned to be the King of Beasts, the tiger is slightly bigger. He's not as noisy, however, and his body is slimmer to help him thread his way through the jungles where he lives. Tigers have to be very stealthy because they hunt in the jungles where the ground is covered with brittle twigs and leaves.

The biggest tigers are those of Manchuria and Siberia; now becoming very rare they can weigh 300 kg and measure 4 metres from nose to tail.

Lions and tigers have mated. An offspring of a male lion and a tigress is called a liger and the offspring of a male tiger and a lioness is a tigon. *Where did you see one?* ....
....Score **30**

Polar Bear (20) The polar bear is one of the largest bears and the most carnivorous. The males average 2 to 2.5 metres in height, but can be 2.75 metres tall, with the height at the shoulders 1.5 metres. When walking they swing their head from side to side in a characteristic manner as if searching or smelling out prey. They have hairs on the soles of their feet to give them more grip on the ice.

The polar bear's main diet is seals, which it catches on land; polar bears aren't great swimmers and seals are much too quick for them in the water. Its two enemies in the sea are the Walrus and the Killer Whale; on land the enemy is man, although it is now a protected species.

In the wild it sleeps in its snow den through the worst of the winter and usually raises one cub, which is very small at birth and held inside the mother's fur with her paw. Has a highly developed sense of smell and is attracted by anything new and curious.

What colour was the fur of the polar bear you saw? ....Score **50**

(19)

(20)

Puma (21) Also called couger or mountain lion. He is a plain greying brown colour; the throat and the insides of the ears are white. Pumas live in all sorts of country throughout North and South America.

Pumas can leap amazing distances 6 metres upwards and 9 or 12 metres downwards.

Jaguar (22) Very similar to the leopard, although he has a larger head, shorter legs and his spots are bigger than a leopard's – some of them always have small black marks inside the rosettes.

The jaguar comes from Central and South America and spends much of his time in trees. He's a very strong swimmer. For his size the jaguar is probably the most powerful beast of prey in the world; he is able to kill a man with one blow of his paw.

Name one other difference between the jaguar and leopard ....Score **60**

Leopard (23) Smaller than the lion or tiger, but immensely powerful. Leopards come from the forests of Africa and S. Asia. Not all leopards have spots – some are quite dark in colouring and others completely black. (These are usually called black panthers). In India the leopard is usually called panther or baghira (remember the Jungle Book?).

Ocelot (24) The commonest and third largest (after the jaguar and puma) of the Central and South American cats. The buff-brown coat, with its black spots and stripes, is very beautiful and the ocelot was sometimes hunted for his skin.

(21)

(22)

(23)

(24)

Serval (25) A medium-sized cat with a rusty-orange-brown coat marked with black spots (some are black all over). Like the cheetah the serval runs down its prey – usually hares, guinea fowl, rodents or young antelope.
Which of these did you see and where?.............
....Score **50**

Wolf (26) Called Timber Wolf in America, to distinguish him from the coyote. Wolves were once found all over Europe, Asia and North America; the last British wolves were killed in the eighteenth century.

Coyote (27) Also called Prairie Wolf. Much smaller than a wolf, he roams the deserts, plains and prairies of North America.

Dingo (28) A yellowish wild dog from Australia, probably descended from dogs introduced there by man.

Jackal (29) I-SPY four species: Black-backed, Side-striped; Golden, and Simenian (a rare species from Ethiopia).
What colour was the wolf you saw?.................
....Score **20**

(26)

(25)

(27)

(28)

(29)

Hyaenas look like big dogs, but in fact they are more closely related to cats than dogs. The front legs are longer than the hind legs, so the back slopes steeply towards the tail. They are scavengers, feeding on carrion and wounded or helpless animals; their appetites are enormous and their immensely powerful jaws can crack the largest bones of hippos and elephants.

Spotted Hyaena (30) a much larger animal than the Striped Hyaena, with dark spots on a brownish coat, rounded ears and a short tail.

Striped Hyaena His coat is coarse and rather long. I-SPY a mane of dark hair on his neck and back, a bushy tail, and pointed ears.
Mine was at .... *zoo*
....Score **50**

Lions (31) Lions come from Africa and India, although the Indian Lion, which doesn't have such a fine mane as the African, is now close to extinction. A fully grown lion may measure 2.74 metres from nose to tail-tip, have a shoulder height of 1 metre and weigh 180 kg. The lioness is much smaller and does not have a mane. A lion's mane is always more luxurious in captivity because it doesn't get thinned out by fighting, hunting and rubbing against vegetation.

Lions are noisy animals; they roar to warn other lions to keep out of their territory; and they move around more noisily than tigers because they hunt chiefly on hard, bare ground.
A lion's tail ends in a tuft. What colour is it? .....
....Score **20**

(30)

(31)

Zoos (short for zoological gardens), were originally places where strange animals were put for people to see them. Now zoos are also important for protecting them and preventing their extinction. Indeed zoos can often be the only place where the animals exist at all. This is because man has destroyed their natural home.

Which animal do you know in this position, apart from the Giant Panda?

....Score **50**

Giant Pandas (32) live in S.W. China. They live in dense bamboo and coniferous forests at heights of 1,800 – 2,500 metres, where the weather is cold and cloudy with rain and snow. Bamboo is hardy enough to grow up there. Bamboo grows for almost 100 years, flowers, then dies. It leaves seeds which take time to grow. Before the forest was used for farmland the pandas could move on to other parts.

Despite years of work on almost 50 giant pandas in zoos all over the world, much more knowledge is needed. For example is the estimate of 400 – 1,000 pandas left in the wild accurate.

Everyone knows the Giant Panda is the emblem of the World Wildlife Fund, an international body which is working hard to save the wildlife of the world and the habitats in which they live. Everyone knows also that it eats BAMBOO SHOOTS, so why is it grouped with the meat eaters? Well the structure of the Pandas and the Bears tells us that though they feed on other things they are closely related to the other members of the Carnivora, from which they have evolved.

World Wildlife Fund has a Panda Club for 5–18 year olds interested in wildlife and conservation, see page 44.

(32)

Pere David's Deer (33) Also called Milou, he is now extinct in the wild. Those you see now are descended from a herd kept in the Chinese Emperor's hunting park near Peking.

(33)

Seals and Sealions (34) fin-footed mammals, are closely related to carnivores, but whose feet have changed into flippers. Most seals have a harsh coat, short tail, hairy soles on their feet, and no external ears. Sealions, on the other hand, have small external ears, a distinct neck, and longer limbs. When on land their hind-flippers turn forwards, not backwards.

Californian Sealion The 'performing seal' you see at circuses. In the water he can reach speeds of up to 20 knots, and he is also able to gallop about clumsily on land. The colour of his coat varies – slate-grey when wet, brown-grey when dry.

What do you see on his upper jaw?...................
....Score **60**

Anteaters (35) The group which includes the Armadillos and Sloths as well. Their special scientific name Edentata means no teeth and although some do have back teeth they are very small and poorly developed. Well, who needs teeth if you live on a diet of ants.

Armadillo (36) The tanks of the animal world; their bodies are covered with extra-hard bands of skin which protect them from their enemies. The armadillo's thick strong front claws make it an excellent digger.

Armadillos come from South America and the southern states of the USA. They hunt only at night, feeding on insects, especially ants. There are a number of species: there is the Giant Armadillo, which can grow as long as 1 metre and weigh over 45 kg. You might also see the

Three-Banded Armadillo, the only armadillo which can roll itself into a ball like a hedgehog; the Hairy Armadillo, pictured here, the most common species; and the Nine-Banded Armadillo.

Which species of armadillo did you see? ....
How long was his tail? ....Score **30**

(34)

(35)

(36)

Animals with hoofed feet are the horses, tapirs and rhinoceroses. Their feet have an odd number of toes; for example rhinoceroses have 3 on both fore and hind feet, tapirs have 4 on the front, 3 on the back.

Here are three types of rhino—two from Africa and one from India. Their horns are not made of bone, but consist of a solid mass of fine horny fibres.

Indian Rhinoceros Heavily armoured, with great folds of tough skin on neck, shoulders, hind quarters and thighs; his body is studded with small swellings, and his tail fits into a deep groove in the armour. The Indian rhino is now becoming increasingly rare.

Black Rhinoceros Smaller, slightly darker, and with a longer front horn than the White. His long, pointed, upper lip is prehensile, enabling him to grasp leaves and shoots when browsing.

White Rhinoceros (37) The second largest living land mammal. He is grey, not white. It's thought that his name may come from the Afrikaan's word 'weit', meaning wide, and that this refers to his broad muzzle and almost square mouth.

Where have you seen a rhino?.............Score **15**

ZEBRA (38)
Grevy's Zebra Largest of zebras, and one with the narrowest stripes. Unlike other zebras the stripes on his rump become smaller and his tail-ruft is shorter.

Mountain Zebra Smallest zebra. Looks most donkey-like. I-Spy narrow stripes becoming broader on the hind quarters, then changing to a grid-like pattern on the rump. He has a fold of loose skin on the throat.

What kind of Zebra did you see? .... Score **15**

(37)

(38)

Cloven feet are hooves with an even number of toes, and these mammals together make up a large group.

Camels do not, as some people think, store water in their humps. Water is stored in sac shaped extensions to their stomachs, and the humps are fat-storage organs which help out when food is scarce. There are only two species of camel:

Bactrian Camel (39) Easily recognised by his two humps and the long, shaggy coat covering his head, neck and back. (This coat falls out in patches during the summer). He lives in a colder climate than the Arabian Camel – rocky deserts and snowy wastes — and travels more slowly.

Arabian Camel Has only one hump instead of two, and is altogether more slender than the Bactrian Camel. He lives in the hot deserts of southern Asia, Africa and Australia.
Where have you seen a camel? ....Score **20**

Reindeer (40) From the far north, I-SPY enormous antlers, which sweep forward as well as upward.

Axis Deer Sometimes called Indian Spotted Deer, or Chital. He is the most beautiful of all tropical deer.

African Buffalo (41) Clever, vicious, and very dangerous. Both bulls and cows have huge horns which, from the mid-brow, sweep outward, backward, and finally forward again at the tips. The coat is smooth and black, the tail is tufted. Sometimes called Cape Buffalo.

(39)

(40)

(41

American Bison (42) Often miscalled 'buffalo'. At the beginning of the nineteenth century there were more than 60 million bison on the plains of North America; by 1889, after hunters had slaughtered them for hides and tongues (considered a delicacy), there were 541 left. Today, carefully protected in zoos and reservations they are once again on the increase.

European Bison Has longer legs and a smaller head. Is now only to be found, protected, in eastern Europe.
What other differences did you notice between the two Bison? ....
....Score **70**

Wild Boar (43) Wild pigs, once so plentiful in Britain, are now found only in zoos, just as well really, since not only are they fierce and cunning, but the Wild Boar's bite (a ripping action) is said to be almost as deadly as that of the Killer Whale.

Warthog (44) This African member of the pig family has, to say the least, a rather unfortunate appearance. He has a squat half-naked body, short spindly legs, a flattened head with a topknot of course hair, and enormously enlarged canines. And, to make matters worse, the male has huge wart-like lumps on his face, (the female's face is comparatively clear).

The warthog likes to live in a large hole. He may dig his own hole, using his tusks to hoe up the ground; or he may simply take over another animal's retreat.

(42)

(43)

(44)

(46)

(45)

Where did you see a warthog or a boar? ....
....Score **30**
Okapi (45) A relative of the giraffe, and not
discovered until 1901. It is a shy forest dweller
of the Ituri region in the Congo.
Gnu (46) Is protected on two reserves in South
Africa. Gnus, members of the antelope family,
are also known as 'wildebeests'. *Name one
unusual thing you noticed about either of these
very rare animals.* ....
....Score **85**

Giraffe (47) A new born giraffe is about 2 metres tall; a fully-grown male may be almost 6 metres tall – easily the tallest mammal.

Giraffes roam the open savannahs of Africa, feeding mainly on the leaves and twigs of acacia trees (a 43 centimetre tongue helps them pluck the leaves from among the sharp thorns). When alarmed they are able to gallop at speeds of up to 48 kmph.

Both male and female have two short hair-covered horns on top of the head; and sometimes there is a single median horn in front of these two. Though there is only one species of giraffe, there are about a dozen different races – each with its own colour pattern. All are basically white, with a complex pattern of reddish or brownish markings on top.

At which zoo did you see a giraffe? ....
....Score **50**

Hippopotamus (48) A full-grown male may weigh more than 3 tonnes, may be 1.5 metres high at the shoulder, and 4 metres long. And his stomach, when fully stretched, might be 2.6 metres long. Yet, even with this great bulk and stumpy legs, he can move alarmingly fast – both on land and through the water. Pictured here is a female with her baby, and below, a male.

Hippos live in rivers and estuaries of Central Africa, usually in herds of 15 or more. Days are spent basking in the sun, or underwater in deep pools (hippos rise to the surface about every five minutes to breathe). Nights are spent ashore foraging for food. When disturbed by a boat, hippos usually move aside and watch – just their eyes and ears breaking the surface. But they are very unpredictable and dangerous.

Watch also for the Pygmy Hippopotamus – much smaller, more pig-like and less fond of water.

At which zoo did you see a hippo? ....
....Score **40**

(48)

(47)

Defassa Waterbuck A heavily built antelope; his wide-spreading horns are strongly ridged.

Nyala (49) I-SPY a crest of hair along his back, and a long fringe hanging from throat and belly. His wide-spreading horns make a single twist.

Impalas (50) Probably the best known of all antelopes. His horns are unusual – they curve slightly inwards.

Which of these three have you seen? ....
....Score **30**

Moufflon (51) A wild sheep from Corsica and Sardinia. The male has huge ridged horns that curve back almost to his shoulders; in winter his reddish-brown coat has a grey saddle marking.

Bighorn A wild sheep from North America and eastern Siberia. His massive horns are curved into a full circle, often more than 76 centimetres in circumference.

Duiker A group of shy nocturnal antelopes, very common in the dense forests of Africa; some are the size of roe-deer, others are scarcely bigger than a hare.

Name two antelopes you have seen at the zoo ..
....Score **40**

At different zoos up and down the country you will see different collections of antelopes.

The Nilgai is the largest, and the Blackbuck the most typical of the Indian antelopes. The Eland is the largest of all antelopes, and the Oryx has unmistakeable spike-like horns.

Primates are mammals which walk on the soles of their feet, have well-developed fingers and thumbs and are able to grasp things with hands (and feet), and the female will usually bear only one young at a time. Most have limbs adapted for life in the trees, though some of the apes, such as macaques and baboons, now live on grassy plains or among rocks.

Chimpanzee Intelligent, curious and full of tricks. When young his face, hands and feet are flesh-coloured, as he grows older they gradually turn black.

Orang Utan (52) From Borneo and Sumatra. He is the only Great Ape to be found outside Africa. I-SPY long, course, reddish-brown hair; his legs are short and bandy, and he is more at home in the trees than on the ground. Unless large areas of forest in Borneo and Sumatra are preserved this animal might soon disappear in the wild.

What else did you notice about the Orang Utan you saw? ....
....Score **90**

Bush Baby (53) Also called GALAGO, he is a long-legged acrobatic member of the Loris family. When on the ground he hops along like a tiny kangaroo – body upright and tail stretched out behind.

Where did you see one? ....Score **25**

Slow Loris (54) His name comes from the Dutch word Loeris, meaning clown, and you'll soon see why. Unlike the bush baby, his movements are very slow and deliberate; watch him move stealthily along a branch, hand-over-hand, with the most forlorn and clown-like expression on his face. His grip is so sure that you may see him hanging by one foot while feeding. Score for the Loris or Gibbon.

I-SPYed one at..*zoo*
....Score **20**

Gibbon (55) The smallest anthropoid ape, and the only one to walk upright – that is on two legs. He can swing from branch to branch at great speed (this is called brachiation) and cross gaps 7 metres wide.

(52)

(53)

(54)

(55)

Ring-tailed Lemur The best known of the true lemurs – which live only on the island of Madagascar. I-SPY a greying body and a striking black and white tail. Most lemurs are nocturnal, long-legged, long-tailed tree dwellers.

Marmosets are dwarf monkeys from the Amazon. There are 33 species altogether. Unlike other monkeys they have paws rather than hands, with claws instead of nails on all fingers except the big toe of each hind foot.

Brown Capuchin From the rain forests of South and Central America. Highly intelligent and a wonderful acrobat; he can leap 15 metres downwards from one tree to another.

What sort of monkey did you see? ....
....Score **20**

Spider Monkey I-SPY a slender body, long muscular limbs and a prehensile tail with a bare patch (like the sole of a foot) on the underside near the tip. Don't be surprised to see him hanging or swinging by the tail alone – it acts as a fifth 'hand'.

What colour was the spider monkey you saw? ..
....Score **10**

The other three monkeys are all Guenons, a large genus of monkeys that live in the jungles and savannahs of Africa.

Vervet Monkey (56) Sometimes called Grivit or Green Monkey, though, in fact, he's yellowish-brown rather than green.

White-Nosed Monkey Easily identified by the heart-shaped blob of white on his nose, and long white sideburns.

Diana Monkey (57) One of the most beautiful of all Guenons. He's black above, pure white below, has a white stripe on his forehead and another on his hips. Look at his pointed white beard.

In which zoo have you seen any of these? ....
....Score **30**

The Barbary ape (58) belongs to the group called Macaques. They are intelligent and have a wide range of facial expressions. It comes from northern Africa but all the other macaques live in southern or eastern Asia. It is large, tailless and lives on the ground. It lives on the Rock of Gibraltar. See page 42.

(56)

(57)

Sooty Mangabey Long-legged, long-tailed and sooty black except for face and eyelids.

Mandrill (59) Very short tail, dull coat but bright blue cheeks, red nose and yellowish beard.

Gorilla (60) The gorilla is the largest living primate. There are two types, the Mountain Gorilla, and the Coast Gorilla.

The Mountain Gorilla, which lives in the tropical forest of the Eastern Congo, is a tailless ape, with a thickset body, weak legs and powerful arms. The head of the old male has heavy brow ridges, small eyes, large nostrils, small ears set close to the head, and is usually hairless. Old males are about 2 metres in height, 204 kilograms in weight, with an arm span of 3 metres; females are smaller. Face is black; hair is black, except for some pale grey across loins; in old males the chest is naked.

Gorillas live in troops of 17 to 30 members in an area covering perhaps 40 kilometres. Despite their appearance they are peaceful animals whose diet consists of leaves and shoots, fruit, bulbs, bark and some roots. They very rarely climb tall trees and hardly ever drink water, getting most of the moisture they need from the vegetation they eat.

The Coast Gorilla comes from the Cameroons and West coast of Africa.
What did you notice about the way your gorilla walked? ....Score **50**

42

(58)

(59)

(60)

Insectivores are insect-eating mammals, small and primitive, who live on insects and worms.

Tree Shrew Thought to be the most primitive living primate – his appearance has probably remained unchanged for many millions of years. About 35 centimetres long, he comes from South-east Asia.

Whales, porpoises and dolphins are a different group of aquatic mammals from seals. Though they live entirely in water, they are warm-blooded and have to come to the surface at intervals to breathe. Some whales have plates of whale-bone instead of teeth which strains the food from the sea. Whales with teeth include the Sperm and Killer Whales.

Common Dolphin has a distinct beak and jaws full of teeth. It can reach 2.4 metres in length. It can travel up to 30 knots.

There are many more mammals to SPY, than have been mentioned here.

Which animal, or animal activity not mentioned in the book most interested you?

....Score **30**

If you are interested in wildlife and conservation and want to join WWF's **Panda Club**, write to: The Membership Department, World Wildlife Fund (UK), Panda House, 11–13 Ockford Road, Godalming, Surrey GU7 1QU. Or **The Mammal Society,** 41 Hatherley Road, Reading, Berks, RG1 5QE. Or **The Young People's Trust for**

Endangered Species: YPTES, 19 Quarry Street, Guildford, Surrey, GU1 3EH. Or **WATCH,** 22 The Green, Nettleham, Lincoln LN2 2NR

THE NATIONAL FEDERATION OF ZOOLOGICAL GARDENS OF GREAT BRITAIN AND IRELAND

NORTH OF ENGLAND

Blackpool Municipal Zoological Gardens, East Drive, Blackpool
Blackpool Tower Zoo and Aquarium, Promenade, Blackpool
Harewood Bird Garden, Harewood House, Leeds LS17 9LF
Knowsley Safari Park, Prescot, Merseyside L34 4AN
Merseyside County Museum Aquarium, William Brown Street, Liverpool L3 8EN
Muncaster Castle Bird Gardens, Ravenglass, Cumbria CA18 1RQ
The North of England Zoological Society, Zoological Gardens, Upton-by-Chester CH2 1LH
Southport Zoo, Princes Park, Southport, Merseyside PR8 1RX
The Wildfowl Trust, Martin Mere, Burscough, Ormskirk, Lancs.
The Wildfowl Trust, Middle Barmston Farm, Washington 15, Tyne and Wear NE38 8LE

MIDLANDS

Animal Gardens, North End, Mablethorpe, Lincs. LN12 1QG
Dudley and West Midlands Zoological Society Ltd., 2 The Broadway, Dudley DY1 4QB
Midland Bird Garden, Stanmore Hall, Stourbridge Road, Bridgnorth
Skegness Natureland Marine Zoo, North Parade, Skegness, Lincs.
West Midland Safari Park Ltd., Spring Grove, Bewdley, Worcs.
The Wildfowl Trust, Waterfowl Gardens, Peakirk, Peterborough
Zoo Park (Twycross) Ltd., Norton-justa-Twycross, Atherstone

EAST OF ENGLAND

Banham Zoo Ltd., The Grove, Banham, Norwich NR16 2HB
Kilverstone Wildlife Park, Thetford, Norfolk LP24 2RL
Linton Zoological Gardens, Hadstock Road, Linton, Cambs.
Mole Hall Wildlife Park, Mole Hall, Widdington, Saffron Walden, Essex
The Norfolk Wildlife Park, Great Witchingham, Norwich NR9 5QS
Thrigby Hall Wildlife Gardens, Thrigby Hall, Filby, Great Yarmouth

WEST OF ENGLAND

The Birds of Prey Conservation and Falconry Centre, Newent

Bristol, Clifton and West of England Zoological Society, Bristol

Cotswold Wild Life Park Ltd., Burford, Oxon OX8 4JW

Cricket ST. Thomas Wildlife Park, Chard, Somerset TA20 4DD

Dartmoor Wild Life Park, Sparkwell, Plymouth, Devon PL7 5DG

Padstow Bird Gardens, Padstow, Cornwall PL28 8BB

Paignton Zoological and Botanical Gardens Ltd., Paignton, Devon

Paradise Park, Hayle, Cornwall TR27 4HY

The Wildfowl Trust, The New Grounds, Slimbridge, Glos.

SOUTH OF ENGLAND

Birdworld, Holt Pound, Farnham, Surrey GU10 4LD

Brighton Aquarium, Marine Parade and Madeira Drive, Brighton

Chessington Zoo Ltd., Chessington, Surrey KT9 2NE

Drusillas Zoo Park, Alfriston, East Sussex

London Borough of Ealing, Brent Lodge Park Animal Centre, 24 Uxbridge Road, London W5 2BP

The Hawk Conservancy, Weyhill, Near Andover, Hants SP11 8DY

Marwell Zoological Park, Colden Common, Near Winchester, Hants.

Stagsden Bird Gardens, Stagsden, Bedfordshire MK43 8SL

The Wildfowl Trust, The Old House, Mill Road, Arundel, W. Sussex

Windsor Safari Park Ltd., Winkfield Road, Windsor, Berks.

London Zoo, Regent's Park, London NW1 4RY

Whipsnade Park, Near Dunstable, Beds. LU6 2LF

IRELAND

City of Belfast Zoo, Halstead, Antrim Road, Belfast BT36 7PN

SCOTLAND

Highland Wildlife Park Ltd., Kincraig, Kingussie, Inverness-shire

The Royal Zoological Society of Scotland, Scottish National Zoological Park, Murrayfield, Edinburgh EH12 6TS

The Zoological Society of Glasgow and West of Scotland, Calderpark Zoological Gardens, Uddington, Glasgow G71 7RZ

WALES

Penscynor Wild Life Park, Cilfrew, Neath, Wales

Welsh Hawking Centre and Wildlife Park, Weycock Road, Barry, South Glamorgan CF6 9AA

The Welsh Mountain Zoo, Colwyn Bay, Clwyd LL28 5UY

ISLE OF WIGHT

Robin Hill Country Parks Ltd., Combley Farm, Downend, Newport

CHANNEL ISLANDS

Jersey Wildlife Preservation Trust, Les Augres Manor, Trinity

JOIN THE I-SPY CLUB

- All you need to join the I-SPY Club is to buy a Membership Book which includes the secret codes. Ask at your bookshop or newsagent.

- Tell your friends about I-SPY. Invite them to join and form a Patrol with you.

- Collect all the I-SPY books—and you'll have a wonderful library of your own.

- Write to me about any interesting discoveries you make. You may win a prize! Remember to enclose a stamped addressed envelope for a reply.

LOOK OUT FOR THESE I-SPY WITH DAVID BELLAMY BOOKS

AT THE AIRPORT
ARCHAEOLOGY
AT THE ART
  GALLERY
BIRDS AND
  REPTILES AT
  THE ZOO
BRITISH COINS
BRITISH WILDLIFE
ON A CAR
  JOURNEY
CAR NUMBERS
CARS
CIVIL AIRCRAFT
CREEPY CRAWLIES

DINOSAURS
FISH AND
  FISHING
FRUITS AND
  FUNGI
GARDEN FLOWERS
  ALL THE YEAR
  ROUND
GARDEN BIRDS
MAMMALS AT THE
  ZOO
ON A TRAIN
  JOURNEY
TREES
WILD FLOWERS

AND MANY **MORE!** TO COME

INDEX

ACKNOWLEDGEMENTS

Illustrations: *Heather Angel*, nos. 5, 9, 12, 16, 19, 48, 56, 58, 72, 74, 75. Zoological Society of London, nos. 1, 2, 4, 6, 7, 9, 10, 13, 16, 17, 18, 20, 21, 23, 26, 27, 29, 31, 34, 35, 37, 38, 45, 49, 52-4, 56, 64-7, 76, 77. *Press-Tige Pictures*, nos. 8, 15, 22, 24, 25, 28, 34, 36, 41, 42, 43, 46, 51, 55, 60. *Brian Rogers/Biofotos*, nos. 30, 32, 59. *Shell Times*, p. 2. WATCH, inside front cover.
Published by Ravette Limited, 12 Star Road, Partridge Green, Horsham, Sussex RH13 8RA ©Ravette Ltd. 1984
Printed by Brown Knight & Truscott Ltd, Tonbridge, Kent
ISBN 0 906710 48 0